USING
SCIENCE
BE A STORM CHASER

By David Dreier

Storm Chaser Consultant: Warren Faidley

Series Consultant: Kirk A. Janowiak

ticktock

USING
SCIENCE
BE A STORM CHASER

by David Dreier
Consultant: Warren Faidley
Series Consultant: Kirk A. Janowiak
ticktock project editor: Jo Hanks
ticktock designer: Graham Rich
With thanks to: Sara Greasley and Joe Harris

Copyright © ticktock Entertainment Ltd 2008
First published in Great Britain in 2008 by ticktock Media Ltd.,
Unit 2, Orchard Business Centre, North Farm Road, Tunbridge Wells, Kent, TN2 3XF

ISBN 978 1 84696 616 3 pbk
ISBN 978 1 84696 678 1 hbk
Printed in China

DAVID DREIER

David L. Dreier (BS, journalism) is a freelance science writer in the United States. He spent much of his career at World Book Publishing in Chicago, Illinois, including six years as Managing Editor of *Science Year*, World Book's science and technology annual. He has also worked as a science reporter for a metropolitan daily newspaper, the *San Antonio* (Texas) *Express & News*. In addition to writing about science, David has a great interest in history and has written a number of historical articles.

KIRK A. JANOWIAK

BS Biology & Natural Resources, MS Ecology & Animal Behavior, MS Science Education. Kirk has enjoyed teaching students from preschool through to college age. He has been awarded the National Association of Biology Teachers' Outstanding Biology Teacher Award and was honoured to be a finalist for the Presidential Award for Math and Science Teaching. Kirk currently teaches Biology and Environmental Science and enjoys a wide range of interests from music to the art of roasting coffee.

WARREN FAIDLEY

Over the past 20 years, professional storm chaser Warren Faidley has photographed, written about, obsessed over, filmed, and somehow survived some of the planet's most breathtaking natural events. It is likely he has experienced more natural disasters than anyone — including baseball-sized hail, flash floods, lightning strikes, blizzards, earthquakes, firestorms, an F-5 tornado and the interior of a Category 5 hurricane. He was the first journalist, photographer and cinematographer to make a successful, professional career storm chasing.

CONTENTS

This book supports the teaching of science at Key Stage 2 of the National Curriculum. Students will develop their understanding of these areas of scientific inquiry:

- Ideas and evidence in science
- Investigative skills
- Obtaining and presenting evidence
- Considering and evaluating evidence

Students will also learn about:

- How thunderstorms develop
- Lightning and its causes
- How hurricanes develop
- Why the wind blows
- Using dropsondes and satellites to collect data
- Wind speed and air pressure
- The Coriolis effect
- The Saffir-Simpson Hurricane Scale
- The movement of hurricanes
- Using radar to monitor storms
- How supercells form
- The conditions needed for tornadoes
- The Enhanced Fujita Scale

HOW TO USE THIS BOOK

Science is important in the lives of people everywhere. We use science at home and at school – in fact, all the time. Everybody needs to know about science to understand how the world works. A storm chaser needs to understand the science of weather so they can track and record the most exciting storms. Scientists also use this understanding to protect us from life-threatening weather. With this book you will get the chance to use science to chase storms.

This exciting science book is very easy to use – check out what's inside!

INTRODUCTION

Fun to read information about being a storm chaser.

FACTFILE

Easy to understand information about how weather works.

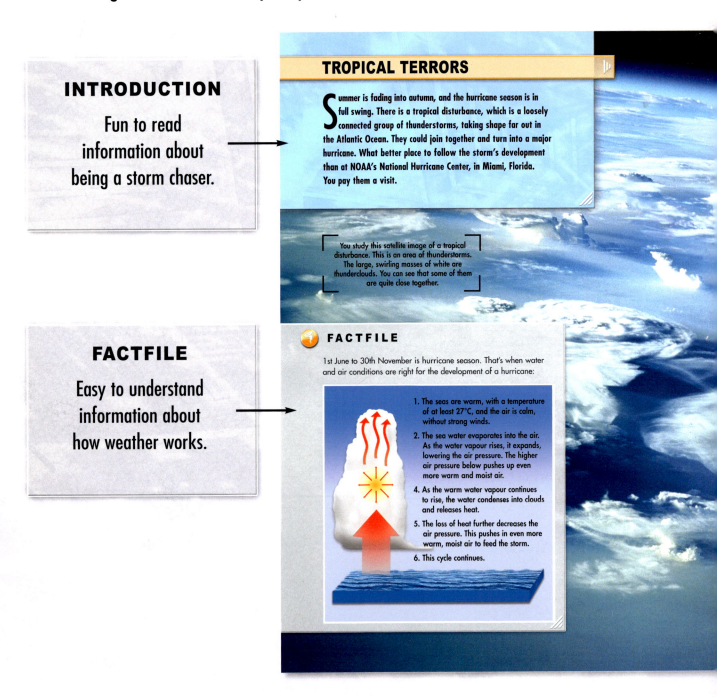

TROPICAL TERRORS

Summer is fading into autumn, and the hurricane season is in full swing. There is a tropical disturbance, which is a loosely connected group of thunderstorms, taking shape far out in the Atlantic Ocean. They could join together and turn into a major hurricane. What better place to follow the storm's development than at NOAA's National Hurricane Center, in Miami, Florida. You pay them a visit.

You study this satellite image of a tropical disturbance. This is an area of thunderstorms. The large, swirling masses of white are thunderclouds. You can see that some of them are quite close together.

FACTFILE

1st June to 30th November is hurricane season. That's when water and air conditions are right for the development of a hurricane:

1. The seas are warm, with a temperature of at least 27°C, and the air is calm, without strong winds.

2. The sea water evaporates into the air. As the water vapour rises, it expands, lowering the air pressure. The higher air pressure below pushes up even more warm and moist air.

4. As the warm water vapour continues to rise, the water condenses into clouds and releases heat.

5. The loss of heat further decreases the air pressure. This pushes in even more warm, moist air to feed the storm.

6. This cycle continues.

WORKSTATION

Real life storm chaser experiences, situations and problems for you to read about.

CHALLENGE QUESTIONS

Now that you understand the science, put it into practice.

IF YOU NEED HELP!

TIPS FOR SCIENCE SUCCESS

On page 30 you will find lots of tips to help you with your science work.

ANSWERS

Turn to page 31 to check your answers. (*Try all the activities and questions before you take a look at the answers.*)

GLOSSARY

On page 32 there is a glossary of stormchasing and science words.

WORKSTATION

The satellite readings at NOAA suggest a hurricane is on its way.

Satellites measure ocean-surface temperatures, which must be at least 27°C to make a hurricane. You find the following data for the Atlantic Basin. This area includes the North Atlantic Ocean, Caribbean Sea, and Gulf of Mexico.

	Water temperature	Wind speed	Atmospheric conditions
North Atlantic Ocean	26°C	80 kilometres per hour (mph)	Partly cloudy skies
Caribbean Sea	27°C	24 km/h	Thunderstorms
Gulf of Mexico	28°C	32 km/h	Thunderstorms

Q CHALLENGE QUESTIONS

Before you can track a hurricane you need to analyse the NOAA readings:

1. Which of these areas of water would be most likely to lead to a hurricane? Why?

2. Which area would be least likely to produce a hurricane? Why?

3. What is the likelihood of a hurricane developing in the Atlantic Basin in February? Why?

4. Which of these water gauges shows the minimum temperature needed for hurricane development?

11

RACING TO A STORM

It's a hot June afternoon. You're driving across the Oklahoma plains. The television mounted in your van is tuned to a weather station. It's predicting a heavy storm season. As rain starts spattering the windscreen, you turn on the wipers. Lightning bolts flash in the distance, and thunder rumbles. But you aren't concerned about finding shelter. You're a storm chaser. Racing to the scene of violent weather is what you do.

FACTFILE

- Most thunderstorms occur in the spring and summer when it is warm. But they can develop at any time of the year.

- The typical thunderstorm is about 24 kilometres across. It lasts an average of 30 minutes. You hope this one will last as long!

You know how thunderstorms develop. They form when warm, moist air rises quickly, high into the atmosphere. There are several ways this can happen:

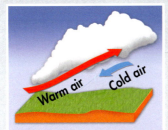

- **Left**: Warm land or sea heat the air next to them. The warm air rises. This is called convection.
- **Centre**: Warm air is forced to rise as it moves over mountains.

- **Right**: When a mass of cold air collides with a mass of warm air, it forms a front. The heavier cold air moves along the ground. The warm air is pushed upwards.

Clouds form when warm, moist air rises high into the atmosphere.

Cumulonimbus clouds are tall. They can be more than 15 kilometres high!

- As it rises, it cools and condenses into tiny droplets. These form towering, flat-topped cumulonimbus clouds.
- These clouds produce powerful thunderstorms with strong winds, heavy rain, and lightning.

Q CHALLENGE QUESTIONS

1. What time of year do you chase thunderstorms?
2. What happens when warm, moist air rises into the atmosphere?
3. How wide is a typical thunderstorm?
4. Where does the colder air go when a front is formed? Where does the warmer air go?

AT THE CENTRE OF A THUNDERSTORM

You're driving through the heart of the storm. Every few seconds a flash of lightning lights up the landscape. It is followed by a tremendous boom of thunder. Your van almost skids out of control! You pull off onto the side of the road. Other vans are parked up ahead, and a TV crew is getting videotape of the storm. Meteorologists (weather scientists) from the NOAA (National Oceanic and Atmospheric Administration) are here too. You join the other storm chasers and TV crews to take pictures.

FACTFILE

Lightning happens when:

1. During a storm, strong air currents cause water droplets and ice crystals to collide.

2. The collisions create a charge of electricity.

3. Some particles become positively charged and rise to the top of the storm cloud. The others become negatively charged and stay at the bottom of the cloud.

4. When enough charged particles are separated in the cloud, those with a negative charge try to 'leap' back to those with a positive charge. This can happen inside a cloud or between clouds. If the cloud is close enough to the ground, the 'leap' may go from the cloud to the ground.

5. The leap causes an increase of electricity, in the form of a giant spark – LIGHTNING!

WORKSTATION

There are many risks for you in storm chasing. Heavy rain makes it hard for you to see. Flooded roads make it hard for you to drive. Lightning can electrocute you:

- In the USA, over 500 people are injured by lightning each year. More than 100 die. But in the UK, only three people are killed by lightning each year.

- The average cloud-to-ground lightning bolt is five to seven kilometres long. Some travel horizontally for more than 80 kilometres before turning toward the Earth.

- A lightning bolt heats the air surrounding it to a temperature of about 30,500°C. That's five times hotter than the surface of the Sun.

- About 100 lightning flashes occur in storms around the world every second.

You watch the sky and monitor weather broadcasts. You have to be constantly alert to the weather!

- If you could trap the energy in a typical lightning bolt, it could power a 100-watt light bulb for 90 days.

- The saying 'Lightning never strikes twice in the same place' couldn't be more wrong. The Empire State Building in New York City was once struck by lightning 15 times in 15 minutes.

Q CHALLENGE QUESTIONS

1. How many typical lightning bolts would it take to power one 100-watt light bulb for a full year?

2. How many lightning bolts occur in various parts of the world in a minute? In an hour?

3. What do negative particles try to leap to?

4. Name two reasons why rain can be dangerous for you.

TROPICAL TERRORS

Summer is fading into autumn, and the hurricane season is in full swing. There is a tropical disturbance, which is a loosely connected group of thunderstorms, taking shape far out in the Atlantic Ocean. They could join together and turn into a major hurricane. What better place to follow the storm's development than at NOAA's National Hurricane Center, in Miami, Florida. You pay them a visit.

You study this satellite image of a tropical disturbance. This is an area of thunderstorms. The large, swirling masses of white are thunderclouds. You can see that some of them are quite close together.

FACTFILE

1st June to 30th November is hurricane season. That's when water and air conditions are right for the development of a hurricane:

1. The seas are warm, with a temperature of at least 27°C, and the air is calm, without strong winds.

2. The sea water evaporates into the air. As the water vapour rises, it expands, lowering the air pressure. The higher air pressure below pushes up even more warm and moist air.

4. As the warm water vapour continues to rise, the water condenses into clouds and releases heat.

5. The loss of heat further decreases the air pressure. This pushes in even more warm, moist air to feed the storm.

6. This cycle continues.

WORKSTATION

The satellite readings at NOAA suggest a hurricane is on its way.

Satellites measure ocean-surface temperatures, which must be at least 27°C to make a hurricane. You find the following data for the Atlantic Basin. This area includes the North Atlantic Ocean, Caribbean Sea, and Gulf of Mexico.

	Water temperature	Wind speed	Atmospheric conditions
North Atlantic Ocean	26°C	80 kilometres per hour (km/h)	Partly cloudy skies
Caribbean Sea	27°C	24 km/h	Thunderstorms
Gulf of Mexico	28°C	32 km/h	Thunderstorms

 CHALLENGE QUESTIONS

Before you can track a hurricane you need to analyse the NOAA readings:

1. Which of these areas of water would be most likely to lead to a hurricane? Why?

2. Which area would be least likely to produce a hurricane? Why?

3. What is the likelihood of a hurricane developing in the Atlantic Basin in February? Why?

4. Which of these water gauges shows the minimum temperature needed for hurricane development?

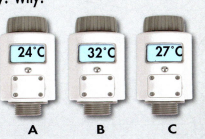

BIRTH OF A HURRICANE

At the National Hurricane Center, you watch as the tropical disturbance becomes a tropical depression. You notice the towering rain clouds and strong winds. The storm is about 1,900 kilometres east of lower Florida. It is moving toward the coast at about 40 km/h. At that speed, it could make landfall in 48 hours. You wonder if the storm will become a hurricane and hit Florida. The Hurricane Center has the data you need to predict how the storm will progress.

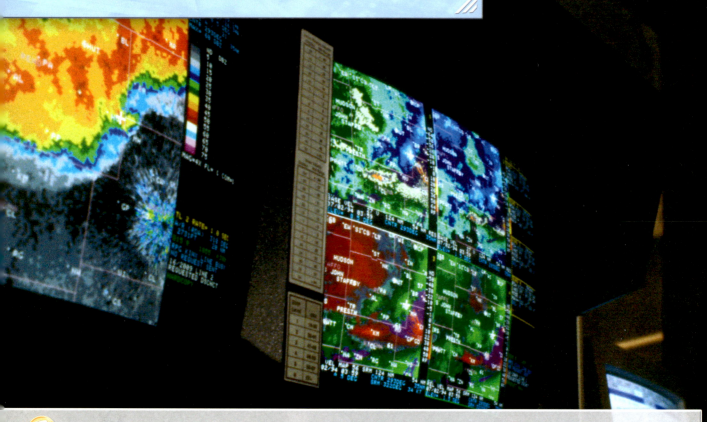

FACTFILE

- Wind is created when air moves from an area of cool or cold high pressure into an area of warmer low pressure. In a tropical depression the air pressure is very low. So, a lot of air moves in to the storm, creating fast-blowing winds.

- A tropical depression will only turn into a tropical storm or hurricane if the winds around it flow at a steady rate. If these winds flow at an uneven speed, or in different directions, the storm clouds will break up.

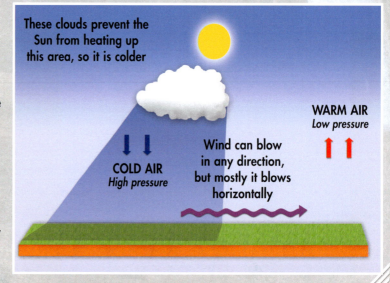

These clouds prevent the Sun from heating up this area, so it is colder

WARM AIR
Low pressure

COLD AIR
High pressure

Wind can blow in any direction, but mostly it blows horizontally

WORKSTATION

Hurricanes go through four stages of development. The stages are marked by changes in the storm's appearance and increasing wind speeds:

1. Tropical disturbance

Air flow moves across sea

- Wind speed 49 km/h or less.
- Scattered storms in one large area.

2. Tropical depression

Air flow starts to flow inwards

- Wind speed 50-61 km/h.
- Large circling cloud mass.

3. Tropical storm

Air flow starts to flow in circular motion

- Wind speed 62-117 km/h.
- Large rotating storm without a central 'eye'.
- Wind speed 118 km/h and above.

4. Hurricane

Eye
Air flows in increasingly tighter circular motion

- Huge spiralling storm with well-defined eye (an area of low pressure).

Q CHALLENGE QUESTIONS

1. The winds in a tropical depression were blowing at 51 km/h. They have increased by 8 km/h. What type of storm is it now?
2. How many km/h does a storm have to reach before it is classified as a hurricane?
3. If the winds around a hurricane blow unevenly, what will happen to the storm?
4. You see these four satellite images on screen. Name the stage of development that each of these storms is at.

A

B

C

D

13**

WITH THE HURRICANE HUNTERS

By the next day, the Atlantic storm has become a full-fledged hurricane. It's now just 1,100 kilometres from the coast. You are with members of the NOAA 'Hurricane Hunters', flying into the eye of a hurricane. Suddenly you're engulfed in the swirling clouds of the mighty hurricane. Over the next few hours, you and the crew use the plane's radar and weather instruments to measure the storm. So hold on, it's going to be a bumpy ride!

FACTFILE

- Satellite photos show only the size and shape of a hurricane.
- Hurricane hunters use an instrument called a dropsonde, to collect data. This small weather-sensing canister is attached to a parachute. It records information about wind speed, temperature, and air pressure.
- The dropsonde is dropped from the airplane. It descends through the hurricane, and radios data back to the plane.
- The data is transmitted to the National Hurricane Center. There it is used to predict the strength and path of the storm.

These planes are above the hurricane's eyewall.

WORKSTATION

Two of the most important measurements in a hurricane are wind speed and air pressure.

There is a strong connection between the two. Generally, hurricanes with the lowest air pressure in the eye have the strongest winds. This graph shows the relationship between central air pressure and wind speed. The data comes from a number of tropical storms and hurricanes. Air pressure on the graph is expressed in units called millibars (mb). Normal air pressure at sea level is 1,013 mb. In really severe hurricanes, air pressure readings can be 920 mb or even lower.

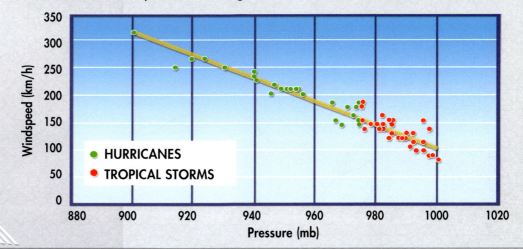

Inside a Hurricane

The eyewall: a tower of violent thunderstorms.

The eye

Wind direction

- At the centre of a hurricane is an area of relatively calm air. It is between 15 and 65 kilometres wide. This area is called the eye.

- The eye is the area of highest temperatures and lowest air pressure in a hurricane.

Q CHALLENGE QUESTIONS

1. Why can't satellites alone be used to collect information about hurricanes?

2. Hurricane Camille, which struck the Gulf Coast of Mississippi, USA in August 1969, had winds of up to 306 km/h. Look at the graph. What was Camille's approximate central air pressure?

3. Can you spot the eye in the main picture?

4. A terrible hurricane struck Galveston, Texas, USA on 8th September 1900. The lowest air pressure measured was 936 mb. What would have been the approximate wind speed of this hurricane?

EMERGENCY EVACUATION

The Atlantic storm has strengthened dramatically. It's now a Category-5 hurricane. That's the strongest kind, and it's headed for Miami. The huge storm is due to hit in about 12 hours. People are boarding up their windows and leaving. You join up with some Air Force pararescuemen to help evacuees trying to get away from the hurricane. Elsewhere, the streets are full of cars heading for the evacuation routes.

FACTFILE

A hurricane wouldn't gain such strength without the spin created by the Earth's rotation. This is known as the Coriolis effect:

- In the northern hemisphere the rotation causes wind to blow anticlockwise.

- In the southern hemisphere, the winds rotate clockwise.

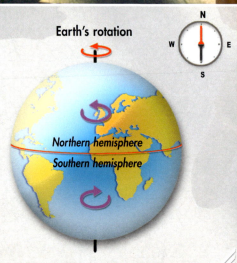

Earth's rotation

Northern hemisphere
Southern hemisphere

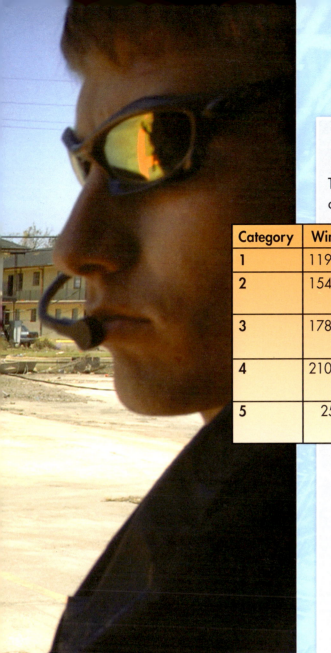

The Saffir-Simpson Hurricane Scale places hurricanes in five categories based on their wind speeds.

The scale also lists typical wind damage caused by each category of hurricane. The categories are:

Category	Wind speeds	Damage caused
1	119 to 153 km/h	Unsecured objects damaged or blown over
2	154 to 177 km/h	Some smaller trees blown down. Some damage to roofs and windows
3	178 to 209 km/h	Some large trees blown down. Structural damage to houses and small buildings
4	210 to 249 km/h	Many house roofs ripped off. Complete destruction of mobile homes
5	250+ km/h	Many houses and buildings severely damaged or destroyed

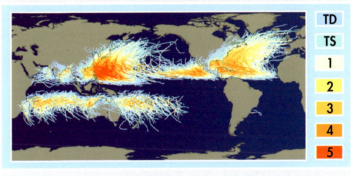

This map shows the strength of every tropical storm or hurricane that has been recorded. The strongest storms overlay the weaker ones. You can see where in the world the worst ones are.

TD = Tropical Depression   **TS** = Tropical Storm

Q CHALLENGE QUESTIONS

1. How much wind speed would the most severe Category-1 hurricane have to gain to become a Category-4 hurricane?

2. What effect does the Earth's rotation have on the direction the wind blows?

3. When the storm you have been tracking was off the coast of Florida, it was a Category-5 hurricane. Its winds were clocked at 281 km/h. When it hit land, the speed of its winds dropped to 201 km/h. What category of hurricane was it then?

4. You have experienced a hurricane in this city before. You remember seeing a sturdily built factory. Its roof was undamaged, but many large trees in the area were blown down. What category of hurricane was that storm?

The hurricane is now beating the city with incredible fury. A heavy rain is falling, and the wind is blowing at 274 km/h. From the safety of a hotel you watch as windows blow in and roofs are ripped off buildings. Trees are flying down the street. Four hours later the storm calms down and you go out. The wind is still violent, at 160 km/h. You're thrown to the ground a few times. Toward the coast the water gets deeper and deeper. Soon it is calf-high. None of this puts you off. First-hand pictures of a Category-5 hurricane are rare, and you want to record the storm for history.

FACTFILE

A storm surge is water pushed inland by a hurricane's winds. A storm surge is often a hurricane's most dangerous effect.

- A major hurricane can produce a storm surge more than 4.5 metres high.

- The storm surges of Category-5 hurricanes have often exceeded 6 metres in height.

Hurricane whips up the sea. Low pressure of hurricane eye pulls up water.

Storm moves towards land. Its strong winds push waves with it.

Flooding occurs on land. It causes more damage and loss of life than winds.

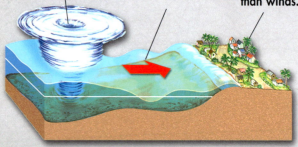

Storm surge

- The biggest storm surge ever recorded struck during Tropical Cyclone Mahina, in Australia in 1899. The surge was at least 13 metres high. It may have been 14.6 metres! After the storm, people in the area reported finding fish and dolphins thrown on top of 15-metre cliffs.

WORKSTATION

As an experienced storm chaser you are prepared for life-threatening situations. You make sure that you have everything on this list:

During a hurricane shops and restaurants close down. Water supplies are often cut off. So you pack bottled water and high-energy foods.

 Electricity lines are also likely to go down. You take batteries, a torch and candles for light.

You might need to drive away from the storm quickly! You carry extra fuel, a basic car repair kit, a spare tyre and a road flare.

 If you get hurt you have to take care of yourself. In your bag is a first aid kit.

You can't walk out into the storm without taking some protective measures. You pack safety glasses, a rope, a water-resistant rescue strobe and a life-jacket.

And finally, you pack the equipment you need to do your job: camera, waterproof camera cover, lenses, flash, and a hand-held anemometer (wind-speed reader).

Q CHALLENGE QUESTIONS

1. You know that you might not be able to return to your hotel room during the storm. What items from the list should you take with you when you walk out into the storm?

2. What element of a hurricane often causes the greatest loss of life?

3. There are bits of flying debris in the air. What do you put on?

4. You can see a storm surge flooding in. You don't have time to run to safety. Fortunately you're standing next to a tree. What do you do?

HURRICANE CHASE

You travel all over the world studying the causes and consequences of hurricanes. Some of them have lasted for seven days! The one you have just experienced lasted about a day before moving on. However, the storm is still causing damage as its tail end passes over, bringing thick clouds of heavy rain that cause more flooding. You rely on your knowledge of the conditions in which hurricanes form. This may lead you to where another one is forming. However, not even NOAA can predict exactly when a hurricane will occur.

FACTFILE

Once a hurricane reaches land, it starts to weaken almost immediately. There are several reasons for this:

- It no longer has its energy source of warm, moist sea water.
- Contact with land disrupts its air flow. When that happens the hurricane's eye fills with cloud and it dies.

Before the hurricane moved on, it threw this car into a swimming pool.

**The world's hurricane zones sit along the
Tropics of Cancer and Capricorn.**

About 97% of hurricanes occur in the Atlantic Basin.

• Hurricanes usually travel west. Then they turn away from the Equator.

• If they begin beneath the Equator they move south towards the Tropic of Capricorn.

• If they begin above the Equator they move north.

• As they move, hurricanes pick up speed due to the Coriolis effect.

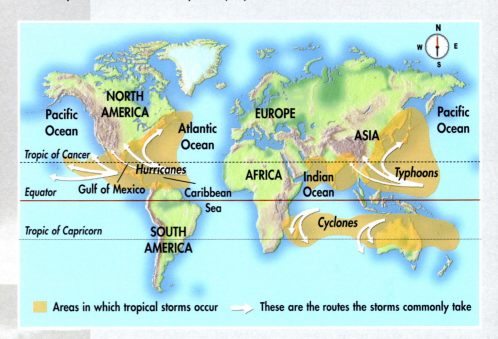

Areas in which tropical storms occur ➡ These are the routes the storms commonly take

Hurricanes have different names in different parts of the world.

• When they occur in the Indian Ocean they are tropical cyclones.

• When they occur in the Atlantic Basin or the northeast and southeast Pacific Ocean they are hurricanes.

• When they occur in the western Pacific they are typhoons.

Q CHALLENGE QUESTIONS

1. What causes a hurricane to die out?

2. A hurricane has started south of the Equator. Will you go north or south to follow it?

3. Tomorrow you are off to study a storm in the western Pacific. What kind of storm is it?

4. Would a storm chaser go to the USA to see a cyclone? Why?

It is now spring, and the hurricane season is over. But this is the time of year for tornadoes. These twisters don't have nearly as much total energy as hurricanes. But they can cause huge destruction in a small area. You want to prepare yourself, so you pay a visit to the National Severe Storms Laboratory (NSSL) in Oklahoma USA. There you check out the latest technology for predicting tornadoes. One of the NSSL scientists points to a radar picture on a computer screen. You can see a tornado developing!

FACTFILE

An important tool for spotting a growing tornado is radar. A radar instrument sends out radio waves. The waves are reflected back by the storm. The reflected waves show the size and distance of the storm.

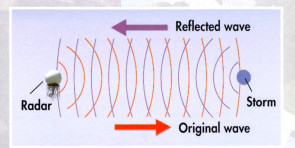

Reflected wave

Radar

Storm

Original wave

Most weather radars are a type called Doppler. They track changes in weather systems. The NSSL's Doppler radar sends out several radio beams at once. In about a minute it collects a great deal of information about a storm.

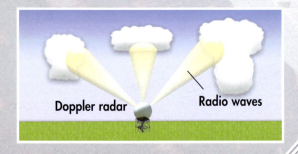

Doppler radar

Radio waves

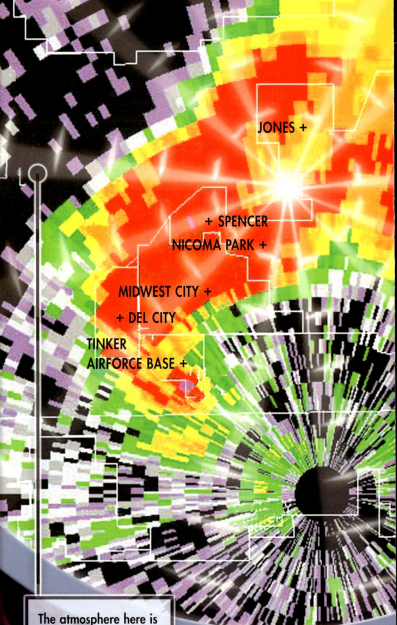

+ ARCHUTA

JONES +

+ SPENCER

NICOMA PARK +

MIDWEST CITY +

+ DEL CITY

TINKER
AIRFORCE BASE +

The atmosphere here is clear of storm clouds.

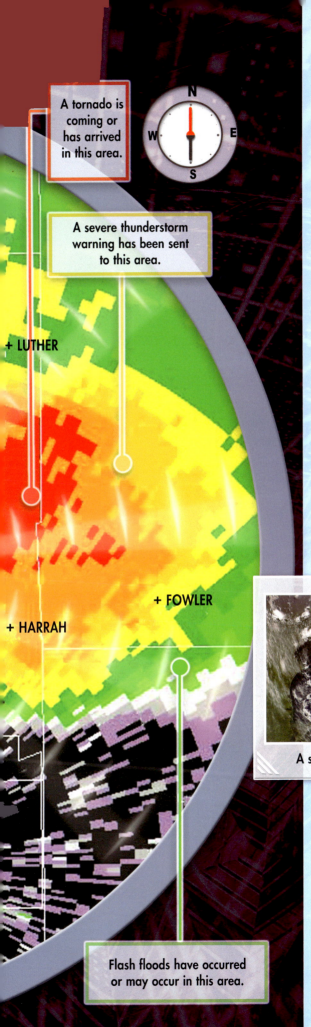

A tornado is coming or has arrived in this area.

A severe thunderstorm warning has been sent to this area.

+ LUTHER

+ FOWLER

+ HARRAH

Flash floods have occurred or may occur in this area.

WORKSTATION

A warning comes through from the National Weather Service. The tornado is about to hit! You race back to your truck.

TORNADO WARNING

THE NATIONAL WEATHER SERVICE IN DODGE CITY HAS ISSUED A TORNADO WARNING FOR...

JONES IN OKLAHOMA COUNTY.

   UNTIL 3.00 PM

   AT 2.17 PM... NATIONAL WEATHER SERVICE METEOROLOGISTS WERE TRACKING A CONFIRMED LARGE AND EXTREMELY DANGEROUS TORNADO 23 KILOMETRES NORTHEAST OF DEL CITY... MOVING NORTHEAST AT 40 KILOMETRES PER HOUR.

   THIS IS AN EXTREMELY DANGEROUS AND LIFE THREATENING SITUATION. IF YOU ARE IN THE PATH OF THIS DESTRUCTIVE TORNADO... TAKE COVER IMMEDIATELY IN A BASEMENT OR OTHER UNDERGROUND SHELTER AND GET UNDER SOMETHING STURDY.

A satellite image of a tornado

- Scientists at the NSSL are always developing better ways to predict tornadoes.
- In the early 1990s, the warning time for a tornado was about six minutes. Today it's about 15 minutes.

Q CHALLENGE QUESTIONS

1. Look at the main radar image. Can you name the four cities which are now in danger from the tornado?

2. If the tornado continues to move northeast, which other cities might it hit?

3. What should you do if you are in the path of a tornado?

4. At what time of year do the most tornadoes occur?

SUPERCELLS AND TORNADOES

You race across the Oklahoma plains towards Jones, hoping to get there before the tornado hits. As a storm chaser, you're in the best place in the world for observing tornadoes. The plains of the central USA are known as 'tornado alley'. Soon you see a towering dark cloud ahead. It's a supercell!

 FACTFILE

- Supercells are huge, rotating storms.
- They can produce heavy rains, severe lightning, and damaging hail.

Supercell

Supercells form when warm, moist air from the south meets cold, dry air from the north.

- The warm air rises over the cold air and creates a circular motion. The air starts to rotate.

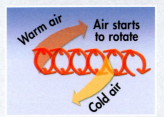

- Then an updraft (an upward air movement) forces the rotating air up. It twists the rotating air into a vertical column.

- The air speed increases. The rotating column of air at the centre of the storm narrows. It stretches downwards. This is a supercell.

- The rotating air in a supercell may then form a funnel-shaped cloud. If that makes contact with the ground, it becomes a tornado.

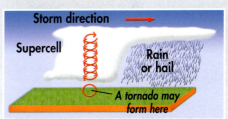

- At the centre of the funnel is an area of low air pressure. This area is called the vortex. It acts like a vacuum cleaner, sucking up air, dirt, and sometimes cows, as it travels across the ground.

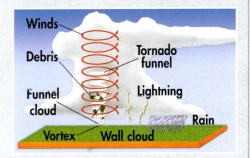

CHALLENGE QUESTIONS

1. What is a tornado's area of low pressure called?

2. What makes the rotating air in supercells go vertical?

3. When does a supercell become a tornado?

4. What causes the air in supercells to begin to rotate?

Y ou've arrived at the scene of the action. A huge supercell rotates in the near distance. A curtain of rain and hail hang beneath it. Lightning bolts flash. You jump out of your van and take pictures. The storm gathers power. Then – what you've been waiting for – a huge whirling funnel descends from the clouds. It's less than 100 metres away. It's a tornado! You watch as it tears an abandoned farmhouse from its foundations and scatters the timbers like matchsticks. Everyone stares in awe.

FACTFILE

Top: Sometimes a tornado may have mini-vortices circling around it, or branching off from it. These can cause a great deal of damage, including crop circles. These are known as multiple vortex tornadoes.

Bottom: On average tornadoes are 120–150 metres wide. They travel six to eight kilometres and last only a few minutes. A large tornado can span 1.5 kilometres or more. It may last for over an hour.

WORKSTATION

This map shows the areas of the world where tornadoes are mostly likely to occur.

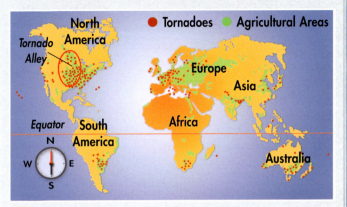

- Tornadoes need lots of moisture to develop. They also need high and low temperatures to develop. These are the same conditions that crops need to grow. This is why agricultural areas often suffer from tornadoes.
- The USA experiences over 1,000 tornadoes a year.
- Most tornadoes occur in the agricultural plains of the USA: Tornado Alley.
- Canada has the second most tornadoes a year – about 100.
- The United Kingdom has more tornadoes, per square kilometre, than any other country. Fortunately most are weak.
- South of the Equator, Australia has the most tornadoes.

Q CHALLENGE QUESTIONS

1. What conditions are needed for tornadoes to develop?
2. Why do tornadoes occur more often in agricultural areas?
3. What kind of tornado causes crop circles?
4. Which hemisphere (north or south) has the most tornadoes?
5. Which North American country has the most tornadoes?

You're back in your van, driving in the direction that the tornado took. You see smashed houses, uprooted trees, and wrecked cars. Even for a storm chaser, this has hardly been a typical day. It isn't often that you're able to witness such an awesome tornado. You're glad you got to see this one. And thanks to advance warning, this twister caused no deaths and only a few injuries. The work of meteorologists and storm chasers is helping to predict tornadoes, and save lives.

LOOK OUT!

The tornado sent a fork flying into a tree. It landed just centimetres from where you were standing. The scattering of objects and debris at high speeds is one of the most dangerous results of a tornado.

The Enhanced Fujita Scale

Scientists use this scale to rate tornadoes.

Category: EF0   Wind speed: 105-137 km/h

Surfaces peeled off some roofs; damage to outside of houses; tree branches broken off

Category: EF3   Wind speed: 218-266 km/h

Entire sections of well-built houses destroyed; severe damage to large buildings; heavy vehicles lifted and thrown a short distance

Category: EF1   Wind speed: 138-177 km/h

Roofs severely stripped; exterior doors of houses ripped away; windows broken

Category: EF4   Wind speed: 267-322 km/h

Well-built houses completely levelled

Category: EF2   Wind speed: 178-217 km/h

Roofs torn off well-built houses; large trees uprooted; cars lifted off the ground

Category: EF5   Wind speed: 323+ km/h

House foundations swept away; cars thrown more than 90 metres; even steel-reinforced buildings have significant structural damage

Q CHALLENGE QUESTIONS

The NSSL has asked you to measure the category of the tornado.

1. As you watch, the tornado tears the roof from a well-built house. What is the lowest category of tornado that could do this?

2. The tornado is getting worse. A car is hurled over your head – it must have been thrown 100 metres! What category is the tornado? What must the wind speed be?

3. If a tornado had a wind speed of 270 km/h. How much faster would the wind have to travel for it to become an EF5 tornado?

TIPS FOR SCIENCE SUCCESS

Pages 8-9

At the Centre of a Thunderstorm

Remember that there are 365 days in a year. To answer question 1, you will need to figure out how many time 90 days goes into 365.

As for question 2: you know that there are 60 seconds in a minute and 60 minutes in an hour. So if you have an amount for one second and want the amount for one minute, multiply it by 60. To get the amount for an hour, you can multiply that amount by another 60 or you can multiply the original amount by 3,600 (60 x 60).

Pages 10-11

Tropical Terrors

To figure out how likely an area is to give birth to a hurricane, you need to bear in mind three different factors. Firstly, how fast is the wind moving? Fast winds can break a storm up, and calm weather is necessary for a hurricane to form. Secondly, how warm is the water? It must be at least 27°C for a hurricane to form, and the warmer the better. Thirdly, what are the atmospheric conditions like? There must be storms in the air for a hurricane to form.

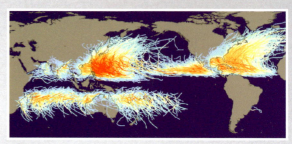

Pages 12-13

Birth of a Hurricane

How can you tell which photograph shows each stage of a storm's development? It's time to use your observation skills! First find a storm with a well-defined eye – this must be the hurricane. Then look for a storm which has no eye, but which is clearly rotating – this is the tropical storm. Can you find another storm which appears to have a circular movement, as if it is just beginning to rotate? This is the tropical depression. The final photo which is left should show clouds which are not moving in a circle at all – this must be the tropical disturbance. The clouds spin more and more as the tropical disturbance develops into a tropical depression, then a tropical storm, and finally a hurricane!

Pages 28-29

After the Tornado

The wind speed of a tornado is estimated after the tornado is over by examining the damage it has caused. For example, if houses hit by a tornado have suffered only minor roof damage, you can conclude that the tornado was probably an EF0.

Pages 6-7
1. Spring and summer.
2. It cools and forms clouds.
3. 24 kilometres.
4. The warm air rises, and the cold air sinks.

Pages 8-9
1. Just over 4 lightning bolts (4.0555).
2. 6,000 a minute; 360,000 an hour.
3. The particles with a negative charge try to 'leap' to those with a positive charge.
4. Heavy rain makes it difficult for you to see, and flooded roadways make it hard for you to drive.

Pages 10-11
1. The Gulf of Mexico, because the water temperature is more than 27°C, winds are not overly strong, and there are thunderstorms occurring.
2. The North Atlantic Ocean, because the water temperature is less than 27°C, there are strong winds that would disrupt any atmospheric disturbance, and there are few clouds.
3. It is very unlikely because it is too cold. Hurricanes need warm air to form.
4. C: 27°C.

Pages 12-13
1. It would continue to be classed as a tropical depression, because its wind speed is still less than 62 km/h, the speed at which it would become a tropical storm.
2. 118 km/h.
3. If the wind blows at uneven speed, it will break up the clouds. This will stop the storm from forming.
4. A: Hurricane; B: Tropical storm; C: Tropical disturbance; D: Tropical depression.

Pages 14-15
1. Satellite photographs only show the size and shape of a hurricane.
2. 900 mb.
3. The eye is circled in this picture.

4. About 250 km/h.

Pages 16-17
1. 57 km/h.
2. The Coriolis effect makes wind in the northern hemisphere move anticlockwise, and wind in the southern hemisphere move clockwise.
3. Category 3.
4. Category 3.

Pages 18-19
1. To protect yourself: your safety glasses, rope, strobe and life-jacket. To do your job: camera, waterproof camera cover, lenses, flash, and anenometer.
2. Water, in the form of a storm surge.
3. Safety glasses.
4. Climb the tree; it's hard to tell how big the storm surge is going to be.

Pages 20-21
1. Loss of contact with warm ocean water; and contact with land.
2. South.
3. Typhoon.
4. No, a storm chaser would not go to the USA to see a cyclone. Cyclone is the name given to a hurricane that occurs in the Indian Ocean.

Pages 22-23
1. Spencer, Nicoma Park, Midwest City, Del City.
2. Jones, Luther, Archuta.
3. Take cover in a basement, or underground.
4. Spring.

Pages 24-25
1. Vortex.
2. An updraft (an upward air movement) forces the rotating air up into a vertical column.
3. When it forms a rotating funnel cloud that extends down to the ground.
4. When warm air rises over cold air.

Pages 26-27
1. Lots of moisture, high and low temperatures.
2. Crops need the same conditions to grow.
3. A multiple vortex tornado.
4. North.
5. United States.

Pages 28-29
1. EF2.
2. EF5, 323+ km/h.
3. 53 km/h or more.

AIR PRESSURE The force put on you by the weight of air. When it is squeezed it is under high pressure. In the centre of both hurricanes and tornadoes, air pressure is low.

ATMOSPHERE The layer of air that surrounds Earth.

CUMULONIMBUS CLOUD A towering thundercloud with a wide, flattened top.

DOPPLER RADAR A type of radar that can detect the motion of air in a storm.

DROPSONDE A small weather-sensing canister attached to a parachute; it is dropped into a hurricane to take measurements.

EYE The relatively calm and cloudless centre of a hurricane.

EYEWALL The circling tower of violent thunderstorms around the eye of a hurricane. This is where a hurricane's fastest winds are.

METEOROLOGIST A weather expert.

MILLIBARS Units of air pressure.

PHASED-ARRAY RADAR A type of Doppler radar that sends out several beams of radio waves at once.

RADAR An instrument that sends out radio waves, and detects those waves when they are reflected by objects or storms.

STORM SURGE A huge wall of water pushed inland by the powerful winds of a hurricane.

SUPERCELLS Large rotating thunderstorms that often produce tornadoes.

TORNADO ALLEY A large area of plains in the central USA where many tornadoes occur.

TROPICAL CYCLONE A general name for hurricane-type storms that occur in the southern hemisphere.

TROPICAL DEPRESSION An area of rotating low-pressure air over warm seas.

TROPICAL DISTURBANCE A group of storms in one part of the ocean.

TROPICAL STORM A large rotating storm system with winds that are not yet strong enough to make it a hurricane.

WALL CLOUD A low-hanging part of a supercell, from which a tornado may emerge.

PICTURE CREDITS
(a=above; b=below or bottom; c=centre; f=far; l=left; r=right; t=top)

Dale O'Dell/Superstock: ofc. Getty: obc tl, 2t, 6-7 (main), 8-9 (main), 10-11 (main), 12-13 (main), 18-19 (main), 20-21 (main), 24-25 (main), 24cl, 26-27 (main), 26b. Oxford Scientific: 29cr, 30br. NASA: 14cl, 23c. National Oceanic and Atmospheric Administration/Department of Commerce: obc br, 13bl, 13bcl, 13bcr, 13br, 14-15 (main), 14-15 (main), 22-23 (main), 30bl, 31bl. Shutterstock: 19tr Piotr Przeszlo/ PhotoCreate/ Magda Zurawska, 19tl Jeremy Smith/ OPIS, 19br Michelle Marsan, 19bl Marek Slusarczyk/ Daniela Schrami, 19cr William Milner/ Arvind Balaraman, 19cl ASP, 29tl Marek Slusarczyk, 29tr Robert A. Mansker, 29cl Laura Clay Ballard, 29bl William J. Mahnken, 29br, 30tl. ticktock media archive: 7tl, 7tc, 7tr, 8br, 10b, 11c, 11b, 12b, 13tl, 13tr, 13acl, 13acr, 15ac, 15bc, 16b, 17c, 18bc, 21c, 22c, 22b, 25t, 25ac, 25bc, 25b, 27t, 30tr. U.S. Air Force photo by Master Sgt. Efrain Gonzalez: 16-17 (main). Weatherstock: 1 (main), 9c, 20b, 26bc, 28-29 (main), 28cl. Wikimedia: 7c.

Every effort has been made to trace the copyright holders, and we apologize in advance for any unintentional omissions. We would be pleased to insert the appropriate acknowledgments in any subsequent edition of this publication.